Still Complete

More funny looks at old railway photographs

CW00376754

by
'Fishplate'

Silver Link Publishing Ltd

© 'Fishplate' 1993

All rights reserved. No part of this publication may be reproduced, stored in a retrieval system or transmitted, in any form or by any means, electronic, mechanical, photocopying, recording or otherwise, without prior permission in writing from Silver Link Publishing Ltd.

First published in November 1993

British Library Cataloguing in Publication Data

A catalogue record for this book is available from the British Library.

ISBN 1 85794 031 8

Silver Link Publishing Ltd
Unit 5
Home Farm Close
Church Street
Wadenhoe
Peterborough PE8 5TE
Tel/fax (0832) 720440

Printed and bound in Great Britain

Cover illustration
Stepney at Horsted Keynes on the Bluebell Railway, 9 September 1962.

A further apology

When we published the original *Completely Loco* in 1991 many people wrote and telephoned asking whether there were any plans for a second collection. Unfortunately, we had to confirm that there was indeed a very real danger of a sequel, but that with the help of our legal advisers, social workers and an eminent specialist we were hoping to delay the inevitable for as long as possible.

However, despite our best efforts we subsequently received a proposal for a further book from 'Fishplate' himself (although we believe it was in fact typed out by the matron at the Home) saying that he had a further 60-odd photos (*very odd*, by all accounts) and would we like to publish them first, or his alternative proposal, a monograph on *Locomotive Tender Rivet-heads of the Easingwold Railway 1905-7, Volume 1 The left-hand sides?*

As many of you will know, by a cruel twist of fate 'Fishplate' is in possession of certain negatives and telephone call transcriptions that make recent Royal revelations sound like a call to the Speaking Clock. As a result we had no option but to agree to publish the present collection.

In conclusion, the proprietor and staff of Silver Link Publishing Ltd would urge you to make every effort to ensure that as many copies of both books continue to be sold, not only to help with our mounting legal costs and the author's ongoing care at The Laurels Twilight Retreat for the Terminally Daft, but also to stave off the day when the rivets once again raise their ugly heads. . .

'And you won't forget to stop at Basingstoke this time, will you? Promise?'

'Then there was one day last week - I must have been doing about ninety down the bank. . .'

'Fancy having to start an engine by hand in this day and age!'

'And to stop it, you just pull this.'

The marriage ceremony didn't say anything about going on honeymoon with a load of smelly old fish. . .'

'Whose Diddums drives the biggest railway engine in the world then. . .?'

'It's quite simple. You light this little wick, then put the lamp on the left-hand side of the engine.'

'We really must save up and get a second headlamp.'

'Congratulations! You've won the Tralee & Dingle's Prize Draw and are now entitled to one week's unlimited travel.'

'Go on, admit it - riding on an A4 was never like this. . .'

'As you can see, it has every modern convenience.'

'Now try letting the clutch in. . .'

'Oh, stop worrying, Muriel. I keep telling you these newfangled contraptions will never catch on.'

'How do you want it delivered? Express, or Fast Goods. . .?'

Some day my prince will come. . .

'Fancy them not telling me the trains stopped running last August. . .'

'Right then, you all know the rules. Out to Fenny Stratford and back, and last one home buys the beer.'

'Sorry, sir, I'd like to help, but we stopped running non-stop in 1898.'

'It's the first time I've seen a pair like *that* on the "Golden Arrow".'

'I'll huff, and I'll puff. . .'

'Don't worry - I'll swim across and get the number!'

'So far, so good - at least I'm holding my own. . .'

'Could you move a bit closer together at the ends. . .?'

'Let them find *that* in their ABC. . .!'

'The train at Platform 1 is for Newcastle. Or King's Cross. Passengers are welcome to try their luck.'

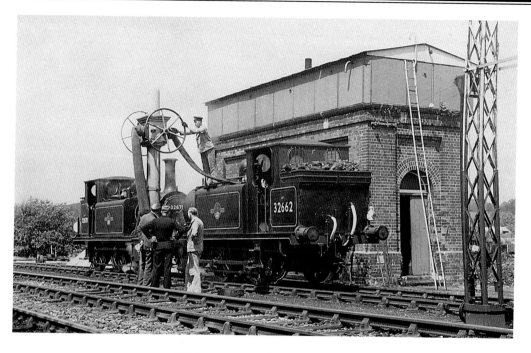

'I'll lay two to one he gets it wrong.'

'If you don't couple it up again, I'll tell!'

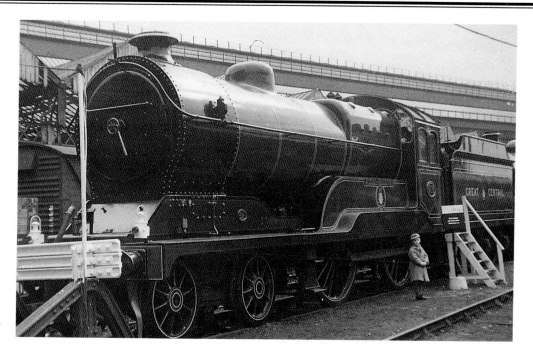

'Hurry up, Dad - I'm hungry!'

'Allo, allo! Will English football supporters please note that a special coach has been reserved for them at the rear of the train. . .'

'Some Eastern potentate or other booked it for his harem. . .'

'Who'd have guessed my experience at Cambridge would have come in so useful. . .?'

'I know we're short of staff, but this is *ridiculous*. . .!'

'*Really*? And how would *you* express yourself if *your* fireman had just filled the lubricator box with sand?'

'If you're looking for that budgie of yours - it went that-a-way!'

'Watch your speed, and don't forget to check your mirror. . .'

'Oh, about twelve miles to the gallon. . .'

'They'd look even better if someone would stop those two goods trains bashing through here every day!'

'And this is one we caught travelling without a ticket.'

'Will someone get me *out of here*. . .!'

'Do mind how you go on the steps. . .'

'We daren't move until Mrs MacWhirter makes up her mind where she's going to sit.'

'Sorry, madam - the rules here are the same as on Irish railways: you can't travel 3rd class on a 1st class ticket.'

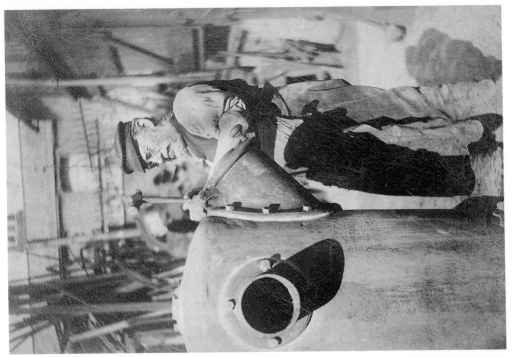

'I'd like to see them invent a machine that could handle *this* kind of precision work. . .'

'Oh yes you can! I've swung a cat in here many a time.'

'And now let us conclude this short service by singing hymn number one hundred and eleven.'

Economies start to bite during Swindon Trip week.

'Come now, Herbert - take your engine out on the 10.15 and we'll say no more about the incident.'

'Are you going to run after her and put the brake on, or am I?'

'Happy birthday to you-ou. . .! Surprise!'

'This *can't* be Selfridges, *surely. . .*'

'Oh, look, Humphrey - I've found the whistle!'

'Typical! The night shift's late again. . .'

'It's a ticking sort of noise - there it goes again! Do you think we should call the police?'

'I *knew* it! Somebody's put a *frog* in here!'

'Henry, for the *last time* - the lamps go on the *front*!'

'It's a sort of two-way insurance. . .'

'Never had it so good! We've even got a piano in here!'

'Just let somebody tell me it's quicker by rail. . .'

We owe you an explanation

Page

47 Built as an 0-4-0ST by Fletcher Jennings (Works No 42) in 1864, *Talyllyn* was later rebuilt as a rather tight-fitting 0-4-2ST. This view was taken at Towyn Wharf *circa* 1913.

48 Ex-LB&SCR 'E5X' 0-6-2Ts Nos 32570 and 32576 arrive at Guildford on the RCTS 'The Hampshireman' railtour on 6 February 1955.

49 Date unknown - except that tea was 3d a cup then!

50 NER '13' Class 0-6-0 No 529 (Works No 1291) was one of 12 that were built by R. W. Hawthorn & Co in 1865. The loco was replaced in 1896.

51 Reflections at Belfast (Adelaide) shed in July 1948. The locomotive is GNR(I) Class '5G3' 0-6-0 No 49.

52 The engine is No 6018 *King Henry VI*, but the location and date of the scene remain unknown.

53 In 1922 the LNWR authorised construction of 60 L&YR-pattern 4-6-4Ts, but only ten were built. No 11114, duly completed in April 1924, was exhibited at Wembley as part of the British Empire Exhibition of 1924-5.

54 LB&SCR 2-2-2 No 122 was built at Brighton Works in September 1856. It was one of a pair that cost £2,409 19s 0d each, and both were withdrawn in the 1870s.

Page

55 West Cornwall Railway 0-6-0 *Redruth*, built at Carn Brae in 1865, was converted to a broad gauge saddle tank in December 1871. Numbered 2156 in 1876, it was withdrawn 11 years later.

56 LB&SCR 'E5' Class 0-6-2T No 574 *Copthorne* was one of ten built to Robert Billinton's order that emerged from Brighton Works between November 1902 and April 1903.

57 No 3T at Castlegregory Junction on the Tralee & Dingle, 27 June 1935.

58 GWR Armstrong '517' Class No 1470 looks spruce on 5 August 1912.

59 Built by the Vulcan Foundry for the LB&SCR in February 1902, the last of 55 'C2' 0-6-0s, No 555 is seen here in LB&SCR goods green livery. The whistle is manhole-cover-mounted, and Furness piston lubricators can be seen at the smokebox waist.

60 An F. W. Webb veteran of April 1872, ex-LNWR 0-4-0ST No 1210 was Duplicate Listed as 3009 in April 1886. Placed to Service stock in March 1913, it retained its Duplicate number under LMS ownership, and served on until 1946.

61 The Welshpool & Llanfair Railway near Sylfan Halt on 2 August 1961.